Welcome to "Proven Secrets to Become Rich in 2023," a comprehensive guide to achieving financial success and building wealth. In this book, you will learn the strategies and techniques that can help you to achieve your financial goals and build the life you desire.

2023 is just around the corner, and with it comes new opportunities for financial growth and success. Whether you're looking to pay off debt, save for a down payment on a house, or build a significant investment portfolio, this book is designed to help you achieve your financial goals and become financially free.

In this book, we will cover a wide range of topics, including creating a budget, investing in yourself and your future, starting your own business, diversifying your investments, and more. We will also discuss the importance of discipline, patience, and networking, as well as the role of mistakes in achieving success.

So, if you're ready to take control of your finances and build the life you've always dreamed of, let's get started.

Written by Mr. John sour

Powered by:

All rights reserved @

CryptonFinance

Contents

Chapter 1- Create a budget and stick to it 4

Chapter 2- Invest in yourself 10

Chapter 3- Start your own business 16

Chapter 4- Invest in stocks, real estate, or other types of investments 21

Chapter 5- Be disciplined and patient 27

Chapter 6- Look for opportunities to earn extra income 31

Chapter 7- Network and surround yourself with successful people 36

Chapter 8- Learn from your mistakes 41

Chapter 9- Live below your means 45

Chapter 10- Have a clear financial plan, with specific, measurable and achievable goals 49

It's important to remember that building wealth takes time and effort, and there is no guarantee of success. However, by following these tips and staying disciplined, you can increase your chances of achieving financial success in 2023.

This will help you stay on top of your expenses and ensure that you are saving enough money to reach your financial goals.

Creating a budget and sticking to it is one of the most important steps in achieving financial success. A budget is simply a plan for how you will spend your money, and it can help you stay on top of your expenses, identify areas where you may be overspending, and ensure that you are saving enough money to reach your financial goals.

The first step in creating a budget is to determine your income. This includes all sources of income, such as your salary, any rental income, or other forms of passive income. Once you have determined your income, you can then start to list your expenses. This should include all of your fixed expenses, such as rent or mortgage payments, car payments, and insurance, as well as your variable expenses, such as groceries, entertainment, and clothing.

It's important to be as detailed as possible when listing your expenses. This will help you get a better understanding of where your money is going, and will allow you to identify areas where you may be overspending. For example, you may be surprised to learn that you are spending a lot of money on dining out or buying coffee, and that this is money that could be better used to save or invest.

Once you have a complete list of your income and expenses, you can then start to create a budget. This involves determining how much money you have available to spend each month, and then allocating that money to different categories, such as savings, investments, and bills. One common budgeting method is called the 50/30/20 rule, where 50% of your income goes towards necessities, 30% goes towards discretionary spending, and 20% goes towards savings and debt repayment.

It's also important to set specific financial goals for yourself. This could include things like saving for a down payment on a house, paying off credit card debt, or building an emergency fund. Having specific goals in mind will help you stay motivated and focused, and will make it easier to stick to your budget.

Once you have created a budget, the most important step is to stick to it. This requires discipline and a willingness to make sacrifices. You may need to cut back on discretionary spending, such as dining out or buying new clothes, in order to save more money. It's also important to be flexible, and to adjust your budget as needed. For example, if you find that you are overspending in a particular category, you may need to adjust your budget to reflect this.

One way to help you stick to your budget is by using budgeting apps or tools. There are many free apps available that can help you track your income and expenses, and provide you with a visual representation of where your money is going. This can make it easier to stay on top of your expenses and identify areas where you may be overspending.

Another way to stick to your budget is by automating your savings. You can set up automatic transfers from your checking account to your savings account, so that a portion of your income is automatically saved each month. This will help you save money without having to think about it, and will make it easier to reach your financial goals.

In summary, creating a budget and sticking to it is one of the most important steps in achieving *financial success. It will help you stay on top of your expenses, identify areas where you may be overspending, and ensure that you are saving enough money to reach your financial goals. By creating a budget, setting specific financial goals, and using budgeting apps and tools, you can increase your chances of achieving financial success in 2023.*

Whether it's through education, training, or professional development, investing in yourself can pay off in the long run in the form of higher earning potential.

Investing in yourself is one of the most important steps in achieving financial success, as it can lead to higher earning potential in the long run. By investing in yourself, you are equipping yourself with the skills, knowledge, and experience needed to succeed in your chosen field and advance in your career. This can lead to higher salaries, better job opportunities, and more job security.

Education is one of the most common ways to invest in yourself. Whether it's a traditional degree program or a vocational or technical training program, education can give you the knowledge and skills needed to succeed in your chosen field. It can also open doors to new career opportunities, and can help you command higher salaries. For example, someone with a degree in computer science will have more job opportunities and may earn more than someone without a degree in the same field.

Another way to invest in yourself is through professional development. This can include things like attending conferences, workshops, or seminars, or earning professional certifications. Professional development can help you stay current in your field, and can also help you build a network of contacts and connections. This can be particularly important in fields that are rapidly changing, such as technology, as staying current with the latest developments can be critical to success.

Networking is also an important part of investing in yourself. By building a network of contacts and connections, you can open up new job opportunities and gain access to valuable resources and information. Networking can take many forms, such as attending industry events, joining professional organizations, or simply connecting with people in your field on LinkedIn.

In addition to investing in yourself through education, professional development, and networking, there are other ways to invest in yourself that can pay off in the long run. One is to practice self-care and maintain good physical and mental health. This can help you to be more productive, focused, and motivated, which can translate to better performance on the job. Another way is to focus on developing soft skills such as leadership, communication, and problem-solving which are highly valued by employers.

It's important to note that investing in yourself requires a long-term perspective. It may take time for the benefits of your investments to pay off, but they will pay off in the long run. It's also important to be strategic about your investments. For example, if you're interested in a career in a specific field, it may be more beneficial to invest in education or professional development related to that field, rather than something that doesn't directly relate to your career goals.

In summary, investing in yourself is one of the most important steps in achieving financial success. Whether it's through education, training, or professional development, investing in yourself can pay off in the long run in the form of higher earning potential. By investing in yourself, you are equipping yourself with the skills, knowledge, and experience needed to succeed in your chosen field and advance in your career. This can lead to higher salaries, better job opportunities, and more job security. It's important to be strategic and have a long-term perspective when investing in yourself.

Starting a business can be a great way to increase your income and build wealth over time

Starting your own business can be a great way to increase your income and build wealth over time. Being an entrepreneur allows you to be in control of your own financial destiny, and to potentially earn more than you would working for someone else. Additionally, owning a business can provide a sense of purpose and fulfillment that can be difficult to find in traditional employment.

There are several benefits to starting your own business. One of the biggest is the potential for increased income. As an entrepreneur, you have the ability to set your own prices, and to increase your income as your business grows. Additionally, as the owner of a business, you are typically able to take advantage of tax deductions and other financial benefits that are not available to employees.

Another benefit of starting your own business is the ability to be your own boss. This means that you have the freedom to make your own decisions, set your own schedule, and work on projects that you are passionate about. Additionally, as the owner of a business, you have the ability to shape the culture and values of the organization, and to create a work environment that aligns with your own personal beliefs.

Starting your own business also allows you to build wealth over time. As your business grows, you will have the opportunity to reinvest profits back into the business, which can lead to even more growth. Additionally, owning a business can provide a sense of security and stability, as you are not dependent on a single employer for your income.

There are many different types of businesses that you can start, depending on your interests, skills, and resources. Some popular options include starting an online business, starting a brick-and-mortar business, or buying an existing business. Some popular online business models include e-commerce, affiliate marketing, and creating digital products like courses and e-books. Brick and mortar businesses can include retail shops, restaurants, or service-based businesses like salons or gyms. Buying an existing business can be a great way to get started, as it allows you to take advantage of an existing customer base, and can be less risky than starting a business from scratch.

Starting a business does require a significant investment of time, energy and money. There are several important steps to take when starting a business, such as researching the market, developing a business plan, and securing funding. Additionally, starting a business comes with a certain level of risk, as there is no guarantee of success.

However, with the right preparation and a solid plan, starting a business can be a great way to increase your income and build wealth over time. It can also provide a sense of purpose, fulfillment and control over your financial destiny. It's important to be realistic about the risks, to do your research and to be prepared to put in the time and effort to make your business successful.

In summary, starting your own business can be a great way to increase your income and build wealth over time. Being an entrepreneur allows you to be in control of your own financial destiny, and to potentially earn more than you would working for someone else. Additionally, owning a business can provide a sense of purpose and fulfillment that can be difficult to find in traditional employment. There are many different types of businesses you can start, depending on your interests, skills, and resources. However, starting a business does require a significant investment of time, energy and money and comes with a certain level of risk. It's important to be realistic about the risks, to do your research and to be prepared to put in the time and effort to make your business successful.

Diversifying your investments can help you grow your wealth over time.

Investing in stocks, real estate, or other types of investments can be a great way to grow your wealth over time. Diversifying your investments can help to spread risk and increase the chances of achieving your financial goals.

One of the most popular forms of investment is stocks. Investing in stocks allows you to own a piece of a company and participate in its growth.

When a company performs well, its stock price increases, which can lead to a higher return on investment. Additionally, stocks also pay dividends which can provide a steady stream of passive income. However, investing in stocks also comes with risks, as the stock market can be volatile and the value of a stock can decrease as well as increase.

Another popular form of investment is real estate. Investing in real estate allows you to own a physical asset that can appreciate in value over time. Additionally, owning rental properties can provide a steady stream of passive income. However, investing in real estate also comes with risks, as the value of a property can decrease and the costs of maintenance and repairs can be high.

Diversifying your investments is important because it helps to spread risk. By investing in a variety of different assets, you can reduce the risk of losing your entire investment if one particular asset performs poorly. Additionally, diversifying your investments can help to ensure that you are able to achieve your financial goals, even if some of your investments do not perform as well as expected.

It's also important to have a well-rounded investment portfolio, including both short-term and long-term investments. Short-term investments like stocks, bonds, and mutual funds, which can be easily liquidated, can provide liquidity and stability in the short term. Long-term investments like real estate, precious metals, or art can appreciate in value and be held for many years.

Additionally, it's important to have a well-diversified portfolio within each asset class. Instead of investing all your money in one stock or one real estate property, it's recommended to spread your investments across different stocks or properties. This can help to reduce risk and increase the chances of achieving your financial goals.

When investing, it's important to do your research and to consider your own personal risk tolerance. It's also important to have a clear understanding of your financial goals and to invest in a way that aligns with those goals. Additionally, it's important to be patient and to not make impulsive investment decisions based on short-term market fluctuations.

In summary, investing in stocks, real estate, or other types of investments can be a great way to grow your wealth over time. Diversifying your investments can help to spread risk and increase the chances of achieving your financial goals. It's important to have a well-rounded investment portfolio, including both short-term and long-term investments, and to diversify within each asset class. Additionally, it's important to do your research, consider your own personal risk tolerance, and to have a clear understanding of your financial goals when investing. Additionally, it's important to be patient and not make impulsive investment decisions based on short-term market fluctuations.

Building wealth takes time and requires discipline to stick to a plan and make smart financial decisions

Building wealth takes time and requires discipline and patience to stick to a plan and make smart financial decisions. It's important to have a clear understanding of your financial goals and to work towards them in a consistent and disciplined manner.

Discipline is essential when it comes to budgeting and saving money. Creating a budget and sticking to it can help you stay on top of your expenses and ensure that you are saving enough money to reach your financial goals. This requires discipline to resist the temptation to overspend and to make smart financial decisions.

Investing also requires discipline and patience. Investing in stocks, real estate, or other types of investments can be a great way to grow your wealth over time, but it requires discipline to not make impulsive investment decisions based on short-term market fluctuations. Instead, it's important to do your research, consider your own personal risk tolerance, and to have a clear understanding of your financial goals when investing. Additionally, it's important to be patient and not expect overnight success. Building wealth through investments takes time and requires discipline to stick to a plan and make smart investment decisions.

Starting a business also requires discipline and patience. Starting a business can be a great way to increase your income and build wealth over time, but it requires discipline to stick to your plan and make smart business decisions. Additionally, starting a business can take time and require patience as you work to establish a customer base and grow your business.

Discipline and patience are also essential when it comes to paying off debt. It can be easy to get caught up in the cycle of living beyond your means and accumulating debt, but it requires discipline and patience to create a plan to pay off debt and stick to it. This requires discipline to resist the temptation to overspend and to make smart financial decisions.

Finally, discipline and patience are essential when it comes to achieving your financial goals. Building wealth takes time and requires discipline to stick to a plan and make smart financial decisions. It's important to have a clear understanding of your financial goals and to work towards them in a consistent and disciplined manner.

In summary, building wealth takes time and requires discipline and patience to stick to a plan and make smart financial decisions. It's important to create a budget and stick to it, to invest in a smart and patient way, to start a business with discipline and patience, to pay off debt with *discipline and patience, and to have a clear understanding of your financial goals and work towards them in a consistent and disciplined manner. Building wealth is a long-term process and requires a consistent, disciplined and patient approach to achieve it.*

Whether it's through freelancing, renting out a spare room, or starting a side hustle, there are many ways to earn extra income

One key strategy for building wealth is to look for opportunities to earn extra income. There are many different ways to do this, and finding the right opportunity for you will depend on your skills, interests, and financial goals.

One way to earn extra income is through freelancing. Freelancing allows you to work on your own terms and set your own schedule, while also providing the opportunity to earn more money than you would working a traditional job. There are many different types of freelancing opportunities, such as writing, graphic design, web development, and more. To get started, you can create a portfolio of your work and begin reaching out to potential clients or use online platforms like Upwork, Freelancer, or Fiverr.

Another way to earn extra income is through renting out a spare room in your home. This can be a great option for those who have a spare room that is not being used and are looking for a way to make some extra money. Renting out a room can also be a great way to meet new people and create a sense of community. There are many websites and apps that can help you find a renter, such as Airbnb, VRBO, and HomeAway.

A third way to earn extra income is through starting a side hustle. A side hustle is a business or project that you start in addition to your full-time job. This can be a great way to explore your passions and interests while also earning extra money. Some popular side hustle ideas include selling products online, providing services like pet-sitting or dog-walking, or even starting a blog or YouTube channel.

Another way to earn extra income is through investing. Investing can provide you with a steady stream of income, and there are many different types of investments you can make to achieve this. For example, you can invest in stocks, bonds, real estate, or even cryptocurrency. While investing does carry some risk, it can also provide you with a substantial return on your investment over time.

Finally, you can earn extra income through passive income streams. Passive income is income that is earned from investments or business activities that require little or no active involvement. These can include real estate, dividend-paying stocks, and rental properties. Passive income streams can provide a steady stream of income and can help you achieve your financial goals.

In conclusion, there are many ways to earn extra income, and the right opportunity for you will depend on your skills, interests, and financial goals. Freelancing, renting out a spare room, starting a side hustle, investing or earning passive income are all great ways to earn extra income and can help you build wealth over time. The key is to find an opportunity that aligns with your skills and interests, and then work to make it a success. With discipline, patience and determination, you can achieve your financial goals by creating multiple streams of income.

The people you surround yourself with can have a big impact on your success, so it's important to surround yourself with people who can provide guidance and support as you work to build your wealth.

Networking and surrounding yourself with successful people is a crucial aspect of building wealth. The people you surround yourself with can have a big impact on your success, and it is important to surround yourself with people who can provide guidance, support, and inspiration as you work to build your wealth.

One of the most important aspects of networking is building relationships with successful people in your industry or field. These individuals can provide valuable advice and guidance on how to navigate the industry, and can also open doors to new opportunities. Building a professional network can also provide you with a sense of community and support as you work to achieve your goals.

Another important aspect of networking is attending conferences, workshops, and other industry events. These events provide a great opportunity to meet other professionals in your field and learn about the latest trends and developments in your industry. They also provide a great opportunity to network and make new contacts. Attending networking events can also be a great way to gain visibility for your business or personal brand.

You can also join professional organizations or clubs that align with your interests and career. This can provide you with a sense of community and support, while also giving you access to valuable resources and information. Joining a professional organization can also open doors to new opportunities and can be a great way to meet like-minded people who can support and inspire you.

Additionally, you can surround yourself with successful people by reading books, listening to podcasts or watching videos of successful people.

These resources can provide you with valuable insights and advice on how to achieve success. They can also serve as inspiration and motivation as you work to build your wealth.

Another important aspect of networking is building relationships with mentors. A mentor is someone who has achieved success in your field and is willing to share their knowledge and experience with you. A mentor can provide valuable guidance and support as you work to achieve your goals. A mentor can also open doors to new opportunities and can serve as a role model for you.

In conclusion, networking and surrounding yourself with successful people is a crucial aspect of building wealth. Building relationships with successful people in your industry or field, attending conferences and workshops, joining professional organizations, surrounding yourself with successful people through books, podcasts or videos, and building relationships with mentors can all provide valuable guidance and support as *you work to build your wealth. By surrounding yourself with successful people, you can gain valuable insights and advice, and you can also gain access to new opportunities and resources that can help you achieve your financial goals.*

Every failure is a lesson, use it to move forward.

Learning from your mistakes is an essential part of the process of building wealth. Every failure is a valuable lesson that can help you move forward and achieve your financial goals.

When you make a mistake, it's important to take the time to reflect on what went wrong and what you can learn from the experience. It's important to understand that failure is a natural part of the process of building wealth and that everyone makes mistakes. The key is to learn from those mistakes and use the lessons to make better decisions in the future.

One of the most important things to do when you make a mistake is to take responsibility for it. Don't make excuses or blame others for the mistake. Instead, take ownership of the situation and commit to making things right. This will help you build the character, integrity and reputation that can help you in the long run.

It's also important to understand that mistakes can be opportunities for growth and development. Every failure is an opportunity to learn and to improve. You can learn from your mistakes by analyzing what went wrong, understanding the underlying causes, and taking steps to prevent similar mistakes in the future.

Another important aspect of learning from your mistakes is having a growth mindset. A growth mindset is the belief that you can improve and grow through learning and effort. When you have a growth mindset, you view mistakes as opportunities to learn and improve, rather than as failures. This mindset can help you to be more resilient and to bounce back quickly after a setback.

It is also important to surround yourself with people who can provide constructive feedback and guidance. Feedback from others can be valuable in helping you to understand your mistakes and to learn from them. Surrounding yourself with people who can provide honest and constructive feedback can help you to improve and to achieve your financial goals.

In conclusion, learning from your mistakes is an essential part of the process of building wealth. Every failure is a valuable lesson that can help you move forward and achieve your financial goals. It's important to take responsibility for your mistakes, to understand that mistakes can be opportunities for growth and development, to have a growth mindset, and to surround yourself with people who can provide constructive feedback and guidance. By learning from your mistakes, you can become a better investor, entrepreneur and person, and you can achieve your financial goals in 2023 and beyond.

It will give you more money to save and invest.

Living below your means is a key principle of building wealth. It means spending less than you earn and saving the difference. This can be achieved by setting a budget and sticking to it, and by making smart choices about your spending. When you live below your means, you have more money to save and invest, which can help you build wealth over time.

The first step in living below your means is to set a budget. A budget is a plan for how you will spend your money. It helps you to understand where your money is going and to make sure that you are spending it on the things that are most important to you. When you set a budget, you can see where you can cut back on unnecessary expenses and put more money towards savings and investments.

Once you have a budget in place, it's important to stick to it. This means being disciplined and making smart choices about your spending. It's important to avoid impulse purchases and to think about whether you really need something before you buy it. When you stick to your budget, you can ensure that you are living below your means and that you have more money to save and invest.

Another important aspect of living below your means is to avoid lifestyle inflation. Lifestyle inflation is when you increase your spending as your income increases. It's easy to fall into the trap of spending more as you earn more, but this can lead to a never-ending cycle of spending and debt. Instead, it's important to be mindful of your spending and to make sure that you are living below your means, even as your income increases.

It's also important to take advantage of opportunities to save money. Whether it's by shopping for deals, cutting back on subscriptions and memberships, or finding ways to reduce your expenses, there are many ways to save money. By taking advantage of these opportunities, you can ensure that you are living below your means and that you have more money to save and invest.

Living below your means also includes paying off your debt. High-interest debt such as credit card debt can quickly eat into your savings and make it harder to build wealth. By paying off your debt, you can reduce the amount of interest you are paying, and you can free up more money to put towards savings and investments.

In conclusion, living below your means is a key principle of building wealth. It means spending less than you earn and saving the difference. When you live below your means, you have more money to save and invest, which can help you build wealth over time. It's important to set a budget, stick to it, avoid lifestyle inflation, take advantage of opportunities to save money and pay off your debt. By living below your means, you can put yourself on a path towards financial success and reach your wealth goals in 2023 and beyond.

Having a clear financial plan with specific, measurable, and achievable goals is essential to building wealth and achieving financial success. A financial plan helps you to understand your current financial situation, set financial goals, and create a roadmap to achieve them. Without a plan, it's easy to get lost in the day-to-day and miss out on opportunities to build wealth.

The first step in creating a financial plan is to understand your current financial situation. This includes understanding your income, expenses, assets, and liabilities. This information will help you to understand where your money is going, and where you may be able to cut back on expenses. It will also give you a clear picture of your net worth, which is the total value of your assets minus your liabilities.

Once you understand your current financial situation, you can start setting financial goals. Financial goals should be specific, measurable, and achievable. For example, instead of setting a general goal to "save more money," you could set a specific goal to "save $1000 per month." This goal is specific, measurable, and achievable, and it gives you a clear target to work towards.

When setting financial goals, it's important to consider both short-term and long-term goals. Short-term goals are those that can be achieved within a few months or a year, such as saving for a down payment on a house or paying off credit card debt. Long-term goals are those that will take several years or more to achieve, such as saving for retirement or building a significant investment portfolio.

After setting your financial goals, it's important to create a roadmap to achieve them. This includes creating a budget, investing, and saving money. A budget will help you to understand where your money is going and to make sure that you are spending it on the things that are most important to you. Investing can help you to grow your wealth over time, and saving money can help you to achieve your short-term and long-term financial goals.

It's also important to review your financial plan regularly. Your financial situation and goals will change over time, and your plan should reflect that. Reviewing your plan can help you to stay on track, and make any necessary adjustments to ensure that you are still on track to achieve your financial goals.

In conclusion, having a clear financial plan with specific, measurable, and achievable goals is essential to building wealth and achieving financial success. A financial plan helps you to understand your current financial situation, set financial goals, and create a roadmap to achieve them. When creating a financial plan, it's important to consider both short-term and long-term goals, create a budget, invest and save money. It's also important to review your financial plan regularly to make sure that you are still on track to achieve your financial goals. By having a financial plan, you can take control of your finances and put yourself on a path towards financial success in 2023 and beyond.

Thanks for reading. We hope you have learned something or many thing and now onwards will try to apply in life.

All the best Mr./Ms. Future Millionaire or Billionaire.

You can put your reviews and give us feedback just visiting at: cryptonfinance.com

Written by Mr. John sour

Powered by:

All rights reserved @

www.ingramcontent.com/pod-product-compliance
Lightning Source LLC
Chambersburg PA
CBHW050319220526
45465CB00005B/2043